'Tis a Gift to Be Free

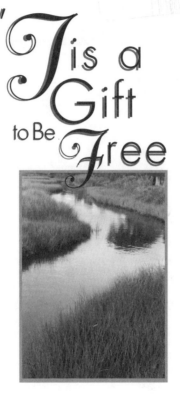

'Tis a Gift to Be Free

daily choices on life's path

Virginia Ann Froehle, R.S.M.

ave maria press   **Notre Dame, Indiana**

VIRGINIA ANN FROEHLE is a Sister of Mercy and the author of numerous articles on prayer and the experience of God, as well as the best-selling book *Loving Yourself More* (Ave Maria Press). Froehle earned her M.A. in English from Marquette University, and now lives in Cincinnati, Ohio, where she ministers as a free-lance writer, retreat director, and spiritual director.

www.avemariapress.com

International Standard Book Number: 0-87793-738-9

Cover and text design by Brian C. Conley

Photographs by the author

Printed and bound in the United States of America.

Library of Congress Cataloging-in-Publication Data
Froehle, Virginia Ann.
'Tis a gift to be free : daily choices on life's path / Virginia Ann
    Froehle.
        p. cm.
    ISBN 0-87793-738-9 (pbk.)
    1. Christian life--Catholic authors. 2. Liberty--Religious
    aspects--Catholic Church. I. Title.
BX2350.3 .F76 2001
248.4'82--dc21

                                2001001198
                                CIP

To the members of my community,
the Sisters of Mercy,
whose support for
my ministry in spirituality
offers me the freedom to write.

Acknowledgments

I am grateful . . .

To Rev. Dan Conlon (Ohio), Wallace and Donna Johnson (Wyoming), Sisters Martha Leis and Rene Mullen (Lake St. Joseph, Kentucky), the late Rev. Arch Thomas (Michigan), and Ema Neeley Wilson (North Carolina) for hospitably sharing homes and cottages where I could write in relaxed solitude, nestled in awe-inspiring scenery.

To Sister Ruth A. Bockenstette, S.C., Peggy McCrosky Grome, Jody Schapker Harris, Diana Jeffries, Sister Mary Perpetua Overbeck, R.S.M., and Joyce Dewald Smyth for reading this manuscript and offering valuable criticism, suggestions, and encouragement.

$\mathcal{C}$ontents

$\mathscr{I}$ntroduction

Overheard in twenty-first century conversations:

> "He's wound up so tight I think he might explode at any minute."

> "If she keeps up this pace much longer, I'm afraid she'll collapse."

> "It's all so complicated. I need to get away and forget everything for a while."

> "Stop, World, I want to get off!"

A song from the nineteenth century plays on the radio:

> 'Tis a gift to be simple
> 'Tis a gift to be free (Shaker song)

Just singing the simple melody of this song gives a sense of freedom, and it reminds us that feeling free is a gift. As we look at the people around us, we see that only some have this gift. How many (or how few) people can you name? It appears to me that those blessed with inner freedom are the ones who open themselves to it by their choices. The gift may be simple, but the choices are not.

This book is about those choices.

How Do We Recognize a Free Person?

I am delighted when I meet older persons whose freedom is immediately apparent. I see it in the way they easily grant acceptance and compassion to others—and to themselves. Lines of humor play about their mouths. If they have ample material goods, they are thankful. If they have only enough for their basic needs, they are grateful. They appear to have discovered that, indeed, all is gift, and they radiate profound gratitude.

When others tell me about the lives of these people, I learn that some have made notable contributions to society. Others have been significant in loving and quiet ways, recognized only by their families or people close to them. When I inquire more fully, I am frequently astonished at the suffering and often tragic events they have endured. They show no trace of bitterness.

They are so comfortably human that they radiate a sense of the Holy in their persons—even without saying or doing anything "religious."

They seem to have found the gospel's "pearl of great price," the "treasure hidden in a field."

How did it come to be theirs? We read in Matthew's gospel:

> The kindom* of heaven is like a buried treasure
> found in a field. The ones who discovered it hid
> it again, and, rejoicing at the discovery, went

---

* The New Testament from Priests for Equality uses the word *kindom* rather than *kingdom*.

and sold all their possessions and bought that field.

Or again, the kindom of heaven is like a merchant's search for fine pearls. When one pearl of great price was found, the merchant went out and sold everything else and bought it (13:44-46).

Have these admirable elders sold everything to become the free and compassionate persons that they are? What "possessions" have they handed over as the price? What did they choose to leave behind so that they could walk through the "narrow gate" (Mt 7:13) into the Reign of God? As I have come to know them, I am convinced that, whatever the price, it is worth the treasures that they have become.

We came into the world with freedom in full measure. We lost much of it for reasons this book will explore. Regaining our freedom is a life-long process. In every decade of our lives, many of us grow in the same qualities that I described in the elders. But many others don't. It is the choices each of us makes that lead us to be more and more free each day, each year, or to remain in our inner prisons.

So I write this book about some of those small, daily choices that lead us or block us from experiencing "the freedom of the sons and daughters of God" (Rom 8:21). But it is also about the price to be paid for this treasure, about those "valuables" we must release from our grasp to make room to hold the pearl. It is about going through the gates emblazoned with the invitation:

> Come! Find that kind of peace which the world cannot give! (Jn 14:27).

The core of the kindom pearl is the ability to live freely in the unconditional love of the All-Embracing Mystery. Its surface radiates compassionate service and peace. Each of us must decide if this pearl is worth the search and its price.

Symbols of the Search

I am intrigued with the frequent use of a butterfly as a symbol of freedom. It is an enticing image. It emerges from a tight prison to fly above the earth. We love the flutter of color when one glides near us, as it gently touches down on a flower. Yet, I consider a butterfly inadequate as a symbol of Christian freedom.

A groundhog or a mole, though less attractive and poetic, provides a symbol with more meaning. In my experience, it is in claiming the earth as my home and myself as human (from *humus*, the Latin word meaning "soil") that brings freedom. In Jesus, we discover that divinity is revealed in flesh—smooth or wrinkled skin, clogged or flowing arteries. Jesus proclaims the holiness of earth, of simply being human. That people and mud are the stuff of the divine is the radical core of Christianity. Our flights of trying to live "above it all," to "rising above" our feelings and limitations, are temporary and even dangerous. We are prone to come down with a splash in the mud, not a gentle landing on a flower.

Theologian Karl Rahner writes, "The real and total task of a Christian . . . is to be human. . . . To this extent, Christian life is the acceptance of ourselves as human beings."

Yet, for the most part, our schools, families, and even our churches hinder this acceptance by teaching otherwise. It is often these institutions that call us to "rise above" our humanness and to refuse to be vulnerable. When they do so, they teach us the "way of the world," instead of Jesus' way.

The Shaker song continues:

> 'Tis a gift to come down
> Where we ought to be.
> And when we find ourselves in the place just right
> 'Twill be in the valley of love and delight.

Taking Risks

Jesus uses the pearl, as well as the hidden treasure, as one of his many earthy symbols for the Reign of God. Although we usually read this parable and compare ourselves to the merchant, we can also read it and compare God/Jesus to the merchant. In this interpretation, the pearl stands for each of us, a beautiful gem enclosed in a rigid, though often attractive, protection. The Holy One risks everything, life and death, to free us from the encasement so that we might enter into the Reign.

As I consider God as the merchant, I propose another image for the Divine: Ultimate Risk-Taker. This face of the Divine will never be popular. Do you know anyone who prays to be united with the Holy in taking risks? We are security-seeking human beings. Still, when has the Surprising Mystery ever called us to a way of security? Jesus walked a path of risks, and the gospel calls us to follow.

The God-Self gives us the example *par excellence* of taking risks. The One-From-Whom-All-Power-Flows eschews the security of absolute control and risks sharing power with and in us. We call our share *free will*. By this power we become the ones to choose the direction of our lives and our families' lives, as well as the course of nations.

The Powerful Mystery risks power in us while knowing that we can use it to hurt ourselves or others. We can harm, even destroy, our planet. We can even use it to turn away from the Divine Mystery in skepticism, indifference, or contempt. Would you, being All-Powerful, take such a risk? Yet, considering all the possibilities, the Gracious Mystery both gives this power and chooses to live with the consequences. Is this not the ultimate in risk-taking?

Various Kinds of Freedom

Politically, exercising freedom is the hallmark of democracy. Maximizing individual freedom while not infringing on the freedom of others is the constant tension of a democratic group or nation. This kind of freedom gives opportunity, though not necessarily peace or joy. Political freedom, as desirable as it is, is not the kind of freedom that this book considers. When Jesus says, "The truth will make you free" (Jn 8:30) and "I have come that you may have joy" (Jn 15:11), he is speaking of another kind of freedom.

The good news of the gospel sets us free from all that binds us from within. As it does so, Jesus tells us that we will be happiest when we are genuinely free to love and serve and that our loving and serving will, in turn, flow into even greater freedom.

Where political and spiritual freedom converge is in recognizing that we are to be servants of no one except *Abba*. In both democracy and the Reign of God, no one has a right to use power to dominate another. We label it injustice in the former and sin in the latter.

Why Do We Not Feel Free?

In the freedom of God's Reign, people give willingly, freely. They serve with the kind of love which brings joy. So why does our gift of free will and the good news not lead us to this service and to this joy?

One roadblock is that, although we want to live authentically in the truth of who we are, we are also afraid of any suffering this might bring, i.e., criticism, rejection, abandonment, or being ignored, discounted, or, in simpler words, not being loved.

This fear of being vulnerable prompts us to build a shell around ourselves to keep out suffering. We prefer to live within the shell's protection instead of in open seas where we might encounter the unknown. We choose to confine our lives by hiding our innermost selves, controlling others, and trying to keep the world around us from inflicting any hurt on us.

Another roadblock: Although the good news of the gospels and the example of Jesus offer us a way to leave our shells, we only partially believe this good news and accept Jesus' way. The degree of our acceptance will be the degree to which we can release control over our own lives and others.

The good news is that *Abba* is the One-Who-Loves-Us with an unconditional and all-forgiving love. Faith in this love makes it possible to pry open our shells, move out onto the open shore, and eventually leave the shells behind. Living in this love gives us the courage to accept our vulnerability, let go of unnecessary controls, and instead, to trust. As we step out in freedom, we can serve with joy.

Who Am I to Write About Freedom?

I write this book's reflections and suggestions for myself as well as others, for all of us who want to follow Jesus' example of living and loving freely.

All I have is the experience of my own search: my baggage at my starting point, the distance I have come, and my path of promise. Here are some of the crowded pieces of luggage I received at birth.

I am the eldest child of an only child who was the daughter of an eldest child who was a very Victorian lady. If you have heard anything about how birth order affects us, you will already guess that I have an over-developed sense of responsibility, as well as many should's and ought's filling the crannies of my soul. Well into adulthood, I combed my hair first thing in the morning even though no one else was around; I replace the paper in the copy machine, the ice cube trays in the freezer, and the shopping cart in the parking lot corral (well, usually). I still buy, iron, and use cloth handker-chiefs, recognizing that I am among a small minority since they are difficult to find. Neither the library nor Visa earns much from me in overdue books or unpaid bills. While I can be counted on, I can unwittingly annoy others with my proper behavior and sense of what is right and honest. I am sometimes a burden to myself.

For those who know the enneagram (a lens of look-ing at personality and spiritual development through nine ways of trying to protect ourselves from suffering), I am a One—idealist, appropriate and serious, with tendencies to repress my anger. A One does not stop with what is good, but strives for what is better or best—often compulsively. Loyalty emerges as a natural virtue. "Wasting time" looms as an ominous sin. I can be an anchor of support for my friends or become a frustration to them. I especially need the people in my life who invite me to play.

For those who are familiar with the Myers-Briggs Inventory (a way of looking at how sixteen different

personality types see the world and make their decisions), I am an INFJ (introverted, intuitive, feeling,
judging—though the meaning of these words in the
MBI differs from our usual understanding of them).
Just one and a half percent of the population shares
this type. (As many as sixteen percent share other
types.) We are creative, warm, organized, and attracted
to the spiritual. Though most of us have a good sense of
humor, we are, at heart, quite a serious bunch. We are
always looking for meaning and striving for harmony.

Persons who follow astrology tell me that my birth
sign, Virgo, denotes perfectionism (did I spell it correctly?), appropriate behavior, and service to others.
Whether or not astrology reflects reality in general, this
particular description fits me.

As you can see, my luggage from birth points me
toward a destination of perfectionism and even self-
righteousness and rigidity. Yet, although I may be fac-
ing that direction, the choice to walk it or to search out
another one to freedom instead is mine.

Some of my suitcases also carry helpful items such
as loyalty, determination, and an attraction to spirituality. Others, like fear of wasting time or feeling responsible
for everybody and everything, are just clutter, baggage
that weighs too much for the overhead compartment.
Flying or walking toward freedom means leaving many
things behind. These losses are the price I must pay for
the treasure I want and also want to be.

Each of our backgrounds and personalities supplies
luggage. It may be heavier or lighter depending on the

amount of love and support we receive or the degree of abandonment, hostility, or abuse we experience. While the stations we pass through on the way to death and resurrection are similar, each trip is unique. This book is a fruit of my continuing journey of letting go of what weighs me down, affirming what frees me to ride or walk faster, and growing to trust Loving Providence more and my ego less. I write as a traveling companion.

If you have read this far, I am assuming that you, too, are seeking the "freedom of the sons and daughters" of *Abba*, not just liberty to do anything. Our search is for an inner, open space from which we can love others freely as we learn to freely love ourselves. I am also, in faith, assuming the following:

- that the Divine Mystery in which we live and participate wills our ultimate good;

- that to be at one with the Divine Will means that we make choices that consider the good of others and ourselves—long-range as well as immediate;

- that the will of the Ultimate Risk-Taker is that we respect the freedom of others;

- that the Gracious Mystery's desire is that we revere all of creation, including ourselves.

Reading and Using This Book

The pages of this book marked *To Consider*, found at the end of each chapter, call to mind everyday situations and ways we hold ourselves bound in our shells. Each of these pages has three concluding parts: *Choosing, Paying the Price,* and *Praying.*

Choosing suggests steps we can take to become freer each day—wherever we are, whatever we are doing. *Paying the Price* reminds us of what we must accept or give up to become more free. *Praying* offers a one-line prayer that can be repeated often to help us live our choices.

I should note that this consideration/prayer process may also assist people recovering from an addiction, yet more immediate treatment for the particular addiction should be sought first. Many who suffer emotional, mental, or debilitating physical illness can still find some inner peace and freedom. Each of us has a center where we know that we *have* an illness, but also that we ourselves *are not* that illness. Therapy and/or medical treatment is frequently needed, however, to find that center. I hope these reflections will open all of us to more freedom in that inner place, even in the midst of suffering.

> Let the thirsty come forward. Let all who desire it accept the gift of life-giving water.

—Revelation 22:17

$\mathcal{O}$pening Reflections and Questions

Believing the Good News

During a recent retreat, Marianne asked me to pray for her. She tells me that she can't imagine how the Creator would ever listen to someone so insignificant as herself, someone who has failed so often. On that same day Sharon revealed to me the guilt she has been carrying for years about the way she treated her father in what turned out to be the last weeks of his life. Neither Marianne nor Sharon is feeling free—although they already know the truth that will make them so. They have not yet claimed their gift. Like so many of us who have heard the good news, they only partially believe it.

Jesus announced their freedom—and ours—when he told us that the One-in-Whom-We-Live not only knows us completely, but loves us individually and unconditionally; that this Merciful One offers forgiveness for all of our sins and failings. This is good news, indeed, and the center of the truth that sets us free.

Unfortunately, some religious leaders have used Jesus' teachings as a way to control others rather than to free them. They propel people into guilt for not following some dictums perfectly or well enough. They give cultural values and standards a religious status, adding more fuel to the fire of guilt. For example, the way women have been taught to submit to men, exhortations to support war if the leaders of one's country declare it, and not questioning authority are cultural values that sometimes get baptized into religious precepts. Would Jesus have attracted crowds if he had been preaching impossible standards or cultural norms and then guilt-tripping his listeners? Would religious leaders have sought his death if he had echoed their demands of authority and the status quo?

Jesus himself radiated the message that simply being human is holy, an expression of the Divine. His teachings do not present a finish line which all must reach or be damned. Rather, they offer invitations toward unlimited freedom, toward fullness of life. The horizon constantly moves, inviting us farther—but into freedom, not guilt. Even the "hard sayings" of Jesus were warnings about the prisons in which we can chain ourselves. Jesus did not speak of offending *Abba* as much as he spoke of saving us, freeing us.

Marianne and Sharon will move toward experiencing their freedom as they can grow to accept and believe Jesus' message. As they do so, they will prepare themselves to follow Jesus more closely as he shows them the way to full freedom. It is the very purpose of Jesus' life to save us from being crushed by the weight of sin and suffering and to lead us to fullness of life.

So if the heir—the Only Begotten—makes you free, you will be free indeed.

—John 8:36

Becoming in Tune
With the Gospel Images of God

Early experiences, persons, or teachings may have left us emotionally out of tune with the gospel message. The way we grew up praying and thinking about God may or may not have been in harmony with the good news—even though we heard the verbal messages many times. We may believe one thing about *Abba* (unconditional love) and feel another (such as having to earn or be worthy of that love). Becoming aware of those places in which our heads and hearts are not in harmony will help us change some notes and sing our life song more boldly.

To note discrepancies between heart and head, consider the following questions. You may want to choose one of them each day for meditation. If you jot down your answers or journal your thoughts about them, it will help you to clarify and understand whatever the questions call up in you.

- Who is God for me? Total mystery? A male who is a father? What kind of father? The ground of all being? The people I meet? Someone with whom I can bargain? One who bestows favors? A watchful judge (one of Sharon's images)? A loving friend? Light or energy? An understanding mother? The center from which all of creation flows? One greater than I can approach (one of Marianne's images)? An all-encompassing presence?

- Does God love me? Does God like me?

- Do I believe that, at this moment, I am clear of every fault and sin for which I am sorry? Do I feel this freedom?

- What are my favorite titles for God? Lord, Shepherd, King, Savior, *Sophia* (Wisdom), Healer, Intimate Friend, Gracious Mystery, Radiant Light, Father, Mother, *Ruah* (Life-Giving Breath), Protector, Master, Gift-Giver, Judge, Rock, You-Who-Are, _____?

- Has God made me, put me on my own, and is now just waiting to see what happens? Or is the Holy Presence with me or in me each minute?

- Does God know everything about me? If so, does God care? Must I attract God's attention? Does God invite bargaining?

- What do I feel that God expects of me? That I enjoy my life? Work hard? Save the world or some part of it? Pray? That I keep the commandments? Make no serious mistakes? Solve social problems? That I suffer? Be grateful? Love? Learn? That I fight against injustice? Accomplish a particular task for which I was created? _____?

- Where is my prayer directed? Up above (where someone is "watching at a distance," as a popular song proclaims)? Within me? Around me? _____?

Our answers to these penetrating questions are so significant that they define our personal spirituality. Our relationship with God, ourselves, others, and all of creation depends on their integrity. So, give yourself time to think about your answers. You may find that all of them satisfy you and seem in line with the good news of the gospels. Or you may become conscious of when your head and heart differ in the way you think or feel about God. This is the first step to begin harmonizing your whole self in tune with the gospel image of God (a continuous process for most of us).

In the section called *Praying* which appears at the end of the *To Consider* pages throughout the book, all of the prayers address God. Most of them offer no particular name for God. Choose the names that define your own spirituality.

What Does Jesus Tell Us About God?

Although she grew up with some Sunday school lessons, my friend Kathy had little knowledge of the Bible and its stories. She was deeply distressed when the evening news reported that the U.S. had chosen to invade and bomb another country as the way to resolve a conflict. In her grief, she felt a desire to read about

Jesus, someone considered a man of peace. That very night she read all four gospels straight through while tears ran down her cheeks. She cried in wonder and love for this man Jesus and his message.

I envy Kathy's experience of being able to read the gospels with such fresh eyes. Yet, it is still possible for those who know the gospels well to look at them anew. When I ask a question and look for the answer as I read, I discover many passages which I hadn't noticed before.

If you would like to read a gospel in this way, you might like to ask, "What is God like?" and search for the ways Jesus describes his *Abba*. Or ask about God's forgiveness of you, focusing on the passages and stories in which Jesus speaks of forgiveness. If you are interested in how the Spirit works in your life, read for all that Jesus says and shows us of the Spirit. (On this topic, continue on through the Acts of the Apostles to see how the Spirit works in community.) As you find your answers, ask how they match the knowledge you had before your reading. Doing so will bring about deeper understanding of the good news and a solid basis for moving on with this book.

Am I Willing to Go On?

John reports several promises that Jesus makes to us at the Last Supper. One of them is the following:

> It was not you who chose me;
> it was I who chose you

to go forth and bear fruit.
Your fruit must endure;
so, whatever you ask of Abba God in my name
God will give you (Jn 15:16).

Notice that Jesus did not promise that everything we ask will be given to us. What he pledges is that any request which leads to making us better disciples, to helping us to bear fruit, will be granted.

Asking to know and experience the Divine Mystery fulfills those requirements. So does asking for a deeper intimacy with the Relational One. So does requesting a deeper faith in what we already believe.

Asking for inner freedom will also make us better disciples. If we ask for it, the Spirit will show us the price each of us must pay. The Spirit will also help us to face our fears, accept ourselves as we are, and trust a Mysterious Hand to hold us.

Are you ready to ask the Spirit to help you uncover your free inner self? What if it means dumping out some of the baggage you are carrying?

As you look at each challenge, you can decide if you are willing to pay the price for the treasure. You are free to say yes or no. The choices are invitations, not commands.

Chapter One

Where Will This Choice Lead? Understanding and Embracing Our Fear

Although we all want freedom, we are also afraid of it.

Whenever I tell a class of adult or high school students that their next assignment is to write about any topic they choose, the room swells with protest and bewilderment—even anger. Students are afraid of not having definite instructions. How will they know that what they are doing will be acceptable, will be approved, will keep their grades afloat or earn them a high ranking in the class? So they diligently try to persuade me to withdraw the freedom and give them the security of rules. Most of us prefer parameters to open-ended choices.

How do we feel about the freedom we have in following the assignment given us by the Divine Teacher? There are so many paths from which to choose. As we make differing decisions, what still identifies us as students and followers of Jesus? I believe the following would provide evidence that we are all still pursuing the same assignment:

- We would so fully love our own selves as human beings that everyone else and all of creation would experience our love. And perhaps others would be amazed at how fully we are living our lives. ("I have come that you may have life and have it to the full," Jn 10:10.)

- People would witness our love as we work for justice and peace in our fractured world. That world may be family, neighborhood, church, workplace, or nation. ("That all may be one," Jn 17:21.)

- People would recognize in us a face of the Divine as the Spirit leads us to become the unique incarnation of the Holy that we are meant to be. It may be a face of simplicity, caring, leadership, integrity, forgiveness or _____? ("God made human beings in the image and likeness of God. Male and female God made them," Gn 1:27.)

Unlike the students in my class, we do find some basic directions on our Universal Teacher's chalkboard. We are, above all, assigned to love *Abba* with our whole being and to love others as we love ourselves. To assist us, we are referred to:

- the Ten Commandments as foundational rules accepted 1200 years before Jesus (Ex 20:2-17);

- the standards for entering the Reign of God which Jesus taught in the Sermon on the Mount. The Beatitudes get special emphasis (Mt 5–7, Mt 5:3-16, Lk 6:17-49);

- the example of Jesus recorded in the four gospels.

But our Teacher and Guide still gives us the freedom to follow these directions in unlimited ways. Of course, we have the power to discount them altogether and refuse the given assignment. With so many options, we are tempted to be afraid. We would like some certainties, some guarantees. No wonder that a deeply spiritual person recently said to me, "I just pray that I am on the right path."

Choosing any direction feels like a risk. It is.

Making Our Choices, Making Ourselves

As wonderful as free will is, it has no meaning and takes us nowhere until we use it to limit ourselves by making choices. Ironically, the choices that limit us can make us even more free at the same time. They create the possibility of discovering meaning and purpose.

What makes Pat different from Chris and different from Terry and different from . . . ? Many things, of course. But we only know Pat's uniqueness by the choices Pat makes—of words and actions. We also know Chris and Terry by what they decide. As they put themselves on particular paths by their major life choices and their everyday ones, these paths provide specific boundaries, structures, and experiences which call for more choices. In all the choices, Pat either draws closer to living freely the self that is made in the Divine image—or runs away from it in pursuit of some elusive security.

Each choice we make limits choices that follow. We fear to lose the other options even as we seek the good of a particular choice. If Steve makes a commitment to a life partner, he limits his freedom to look around for another. Yet it frees the two of them to pursue the deepest intimacy and sharing of which they are capable. If Sarah chooses a hobby, job, or profession, she limits pursuing many other possibilities at the same time. Yet her decision provides the freedom to work toward competence, excellence, or the satisfaction of some accomplishment. If I decide to vacation in the mountains, I will forego the ocean or the museums or the night life of a city. You are free to spend the next few minutes in quiet prayer, but you must choose between doing so or continuing to read this book. (I trust that either choice is good.)

One thing is certain: While a choice may lead to stunning vistas and quiet, peaceful streams, it will also present roads filled with brambles and potentially dangerous side paths. The traveler will have to climb cliffs, endure the thirst of deserts, and struggle through storms. For example, one's partner may have undesirable traits not fully recognized (love being blind) before the commitment. Financial problems may be over-whelming. An impaired child may be born. The job may be overly stressful or taken away. Rain may fall during the whole vacation. Prayer may be a struggle with distractions at a time when we hoped for some consolation.

Drifting, not making decisions, can be tempting. But drifting is also a choice, and it is usually a detri-mental one. Unless we make conscious decisions and accept responsibility for them, we do not become mature sons and daughters of the Ultimate Risk-Taker. In making choices, we co-create our world with the Creative Power and, thereby, grow more into our divine image and likeness.

Fear That Our Choices Will Bind Us Rather Than Free Us

Despite free will, it is not unusual for people to find themselves feeling bound and chained by their choices rather than rejoicing in their freedom. They may feel overwhelmed with the burdens and responsibilities they have undertaken. How many spouses have not had times when they felt a desire to be single and "free" again? Who hasn't wanted to bolt from a demanding job? A minister friend confided that, during one year in his mid-life, he was bombarded with fan-tasies of driving to the expressway, parking his car, and thumbing his way to anywhere. At these times, we ask the Embracing Mystery to hold on to us and lead us to a path which will bring us to the inner peace and freedom we desire. We ask for the courage to make the choices that will awaken, nourish, or free a burdened inner self.

When I was a young adult, choosing my life direction, I prayed that an angel or saint would just appear and tell me what to do. I also suggested to these heavenly powers, after no such thing happened, that I'd settle for just a sign. I wanted so much to be certain that I was doing "what I am supposed to do," as if only one path could lead me to Embracing Love. I misinterpreted my freedom as a daughter of *Abba*. I did not realize that Unconditional Love would be with me no matter which way I chose to walk. Some paths might lead more directly to my becoming the person whom the Providential One wants me to be, but I had yet to learn that the Spirit would lead me in that direction no matter which choice I made.

Only one thing can give us the courage to make the major choices of our lives thoughtfully, passionately, and courageously. Only one thing can propel us to make our secondary choices and our day-by-day ones with confidence and freedom, and that is *believing the good news*.

Do we believe what Jesus tells us about *Abba*, that we dwell in a Saving Mystery who loves us and cares for us so totally that the very hairs on our head are numbered (Lk 12:7)? Can we trust the Forgiving Mystery described in the story of the father and his prodigal son (Lk 15:11-32)? Do we believe that the

Hound of Heaven chases after us like the woman who searches for the coin or the shepherd who trails the lost sheep (Lk 15:4-10)?

Of course our decisions may result in suffering—intentionally or not—for ourselves or another. We have reason to fear. Every choice is a risk, just as sharing with us the power to choose is the great gamble of the Divine Risk-Taker. But our safety net is the Forgiving Mystery which wraps itself around us in our sorrow or failure. It is a Presence that keeps the promise: "Know that I am with you always" (Mt 28:20). It is knowing that no matter what happens, the door to inner freedom is still open.

Jesus tells us,

> "People who are healthy don't need a doctor;
> sick ones do.
> I have come to call sinners,
> not the righteous" (Mk 2:17).

I invite you to reflect on the following considerations on risk-taking.

TO CONSIDER

Mahatma Gandhi wrote: "Freedom is not worth having if it does not include the freedom to make mistakes."

Although we *know* that the Ultimate Risk-Taker does not give us freedom just to censor us if we do something wrong, and although we *know* that deciding for any one of many choices may be okay, some of us may not *feel* like *Abba* is so unconditionally loving. Potential mistakes can loom as potential tragedies. Sometimes these feelings are confirmed in work places where mistakes mean censure, demotion, or wage loss.

Fear of a "mistaken" choice can be paralyzing. We know from experience that unexpected circumstances can prompt us to regret a decision. Then we experience feelings that vary from disappointment to profound hurt to guilt. Fear of suffering these feelings often goes along with making our choices.

Some people's fear sends them drifting in a wasteland of indecision. Some abort their fear and discomfort by leaping into a decision without enough consideration. Some squash their fear within and do not listen to what helpful things it might be saying.

Fear is a part of all of us, of our humanness. But we are not our fear. We can accept it and the suffering it entails, remembering it is only one part of us. When we experience fear and still move ahead, still make choices, we become courageous and we strengthen that part of ourselves called trust.

Can I accept my feeling of fear and still make choices with faith in the Giving Mystery who breathes me into life and freedom?

Choosing: I will be aware of any fear I feel in making a decision—big or small. I will accept it and listen to what it is saying.

Paying the Price: I will let the fear dwell in my body for a few minutes and acknowledge it as a part of me.

Praying: Help me to receive my fear and then to release it to you.

TO CONSIDER

> "There is nothing final about a mistake, except
> its being taken as final."
>
> —Phyllis Bottome

My friend Patrice is an artist. She assures me, "There are no mistakes. Everything can be made into something else or used in another way." When she shows me her splendid, sculptured paintings, she can point out places where she has transformed "mistakes" into strong and compelling images.

How do I handle the fear I feel about making a "mistaken" decision? Do I acknowledge it? Push it down? Deny it? Seek security in food, alcohol, overwork, sex, or compulsive talking?

Can I recall a time when a "mistake" turned into a blessing?

Choosing: When I make "mistakes" today (and who will not?), I will creatively search for a good that comes from them. The good may be outside or inside of me.

Paying the Price: I will accept any feelings that flow from my "mistakes."

Praying: Help me to know that my "mistakes" just reveal me as a human being—like everyone else.

To Consider

Jesus says that it is "faith that saves you" (Lk 7:50). Faith is like the mustard seed in Jesus' parable (Lk 13:18-19). It begins as a seed and grows to a tree of great fullness. Gradually. Over the years.

What waters and fertilizes it? The Spirit—when we ask for its growth. Our actions—when we accept our fears but act in faith and trust.

We can also grow in faith by remembering with Paul,

What will separate us from the love of Christ?
Trouble? Calamity? Persecution? Hunger?
Nakedness? Danger? Violence? . . .
Yet, in all these we are more than conquerors
because of God who has loved us.
For I am certain that neither death nor life,
neither angels nor demons,
neither the present nor the future,
neither heights nor depths—
nor anything else in all creation—
will be able to separate us from the love of God
that comes to us in Christ Jesus, our Savior
(Rom 8:35-39).

When we are certain that nothing can separate us from Ultimate Good, that love is stronger than any suffering, we can risk anything. When we find our own courage, we not only experience a part of

God's Reign in our hearts, but we also become a shelter for others seeking enough strength to take risks. Like the tree in the parable, we can support them in our branches as they renew their courage (Mk 4:30-32).

> *Choosing:* I will take some risk today: try a new food; introduce myself to someone I have seen but never spoken with; listen to a person or read an article with ideas that seem opposed to mine; take a drive to an area unknown to me, or take a walk in a neighborhood quite different from one of my own economic or social class; ask someone what he or she believes about God; ask someone if he or she believes in miracles or the death penalty or the value of sports, etc.

> *Paying the Price:* I may feel the hurt of refusal, rejection, or being ignored.

> *Praying:* Increase my trust that you are with me no matter what happens.

Chapter Two

Wrapping a Shell Around the Pearl

Each of us enters the world as a beautiful pearl—not a perfect one (no pearls are perfect), but as a wonderful gem with its own radiance and iridescence. The pearl has developed from friction, from the sufferings of our ancestors and their triumphs over them. Their evolution and growth is integrated into the uniqueness of each of us.

Consider how we "ooh" and "aah" over a newborn and how excited we are about its life. We love the baby precisely because it is so vulnerable and dependent on us. It calls out our protective and nurturing qualities. When we were born, others felt this way about us. Yet, quite early in life, even in the best of situations, we experienced the hurt that comes from our vulnerability as those who cared for us were unable to meet all of our needs or understand us completely or protect us from all pain. This may or may not have been the fault of our caretakers. We came into an imperfect world that could

43

not care for us perfectly. We felt hurt or afraid or angry or sad or abandoned.

Early on we began to pull something around ourselves to feel less vulnerable, to protect ourselves from the suffering. We began to develop a shell. At some, perhaps subconscious, level we may even have felt that, if we etched a particularly attractive pattern on it, we would be safe and loved.

We may try to design the pattern according to what we perceived was expected of us in childhood; for example, not making mistakes; being independent (not having any needs which may inconvenience others); always being cheerful and making people laugh. Act tough (showing feelings is weak); always be nice and do what makes others happy; don't be angry; make sure whatever you do is a success. Don't let yourself feel afraid; act as if you "have it all together." Keep all of the rules; don't let anyone play you for a fool—always know what is going on. These behaviors may or may not have been taught to us directly, but they are the values of "the world" carried in our society, churches, and families. We absorb some of their patterns. We etch them into the shell, the part of ourselves which we present to others.

We not only cover our shells with such patterns, we may even want to believe that they are our true selves. Should anyone challenge them, watch us defend and attack. We can manage all sorts of inner ruses to keep the truth at bay. Crouching within our shells feels more secure than letting others know they have touched on the truth. Our shells, however, manage to prevent or impair the honest relationships and intimacy that bring joy and characterize the Community of God. Jesus invites us to leave our shells and come to his table so that we might be free enough to experience fullness of life.

The considerations that follow call us to reflect on some of the behaviors that flow from patterns we have etched. They also suggest ways to erase them, if we are willing to risk.

To Consider

Some shells are etched with a pattern of independence that signals, "I don't need anything." Needing others leaves us open to hurt. What if the other cannot give us what we need, or worse, refuses to do so? What if the other person discounts us by acting as if our request is not important or is a bother—even if he or she does supply the help?

Our needs may be as small as Kate's, who was thirsty when she and a friend were visiting a sick neighbor. "I didn't want to interrupt the conversation," she says, still thirsty after she leaves. Or as medium as Ada's desire to continue attending church on Sunday although she has had to give up driving. She won't ask for a ride. "I don't want to bother anyone," she explains. Or they may be as serious as Jake's needing financial help to pay the mortgage this month. "I don't ask for no help from nobody," he says, putting himself into further jeopardy.

Am I afraid to ask for what I need, small, medium, or large? If so, what do I most fear about doing so?

When have others unexpectedly met my desires after I hesitated to ask? When were my needs ignored?

Can I handle again the hurt of refusal? Or do I decide to keep my needs behind my shell?

Choosing: I will ask someone to do something for me; for example, bring me a glass of water, drop some mail at the post office, make a telephone call, lend me an item, watch the children or a pet for a brief period. Or I will seek help on a project. If I need to think out loud as I make a decision, I will ask someone to listen to me.

Paying the Price: I may feel hurt from a refusal or an ungracious response.

Praying: Help me to know that I, like all human beings, need help, respect, and acceptance from others.

To Consider

We accept our humanity—and therefore, our divinity—when we accept the vulnerability that comes from having needs. We live on the inside of our shells when we deprive ourselves of what we need or want, fearing that no one else would care enough to help us. Or worse, when we fear others might judge us as weak.

Jesus needed friends, emotional support (Mk 3:14, Lk 10:38), as well as financial help (Lk 8:3). Sometimes he received what he needed and sometimes he suffered the sting of asking for it and not receiving it.

If we want to be followers of Jesus, we will not only accept our needs but, like him, ask others for help. We must be prepared, however, to accept the suffering of refusal just as he did. We need friends, yet we must be willing to risk betrayal as he did—or no genuine friendship can develop. We need emotional support, yet we may also experience, as Jesus did, that some people do not have enough understanding to walk with us.

Choosing: I will read a Bible passage about Jesus and his needs.

Paying the Price: Taking the time to read.

Praying: Help me to recognize my needs and rejoice in being human.

To Consider

Women can be especially high in reluctance to "bothering anyone." Just ask women at a gathering how many would like a cup of coffee. Then, as you go to fill your coffee maker, mention that it will be ready in a few minutes. Prepare for a chorus of "Oh, don't bother. I'll take instant." As if you had to go to Jamaica to pick the beans!

Women are still often socialized against taking care of personal or physical needs, and are given messages that tell them not to "be a bother" to anyone. The accusation *selfish* erupts within many women when they begin to satisfy their own desires or permit someone else to "go out of their way" for them. Some sketch an attractive shell design showing themselves as serving others and never thinking of self. It is a design that wins praise. Yet, if someone must always serve others and can't let others serve her, she will ache with an empty space from unmet needs within her. She may try to get the emptiness filled by laying guilt on those she helps, by proclaiming how much she does for others and how little others appreciate it. People will eventually see the word *martyr* scrawled over her shell design.

While adopting a shell of constant service is more common for women, some men also live behind a shell of care-taking. They may feel it is a weakness to have needs and ask for help for themselves.

Choosing: If someone needs help, I will notice whether I respond freely (am able to say yes or no), or if I am compelled to say yes. The next time that I need some help, I will notice how I feel about asking for it.

Paying the Price: If I am usually compelled to say yes and I decide to say no, I may feel guilty. If I ask for help, I may feel hurt if I am refused or helped ungraciously.

Praying: Help me to lovingly embrace any of my needs that may surface today.

To Consider

Usually men are more socialized to independence from emotional expression, although some women also find themselves projecting the lower jaw and refusing to ask for support.

Everyone needs emotional support to get through major crises like death, losing a job, rejection from a loved one, or becoming disabled in some way. When we need support and understanding and think, "No one could understand anyway," or, "I might cry and the person will think I am weak," we will probably suffer the sadness and grief much longer.

We also fare much better when we have support for daily problems: a harried day at work, stress from caring for squabbling children, a car or appliance breakdown, feeling overwhelmed with too much to do. A person with the shell of independence will square shoulders and look straight ahead instead of asking for support. Such persons have also been known to explode with displaced anger at others who have nothing to do with the problem.

Jesus is our model of accepting our emotional needs. He surrounded himself with friends because he needed human support for himself and for his ministry. He went to Martha, Mary, and Lazarus because he needed a haven of acceptance and relaxation (Lk 10:13). He went often to the mountaintop because he needed to be with his *Abba* (Lk

9:28). He felt hurt when his friends didn't stay awake after he'd asked them to watch with him (Mt 26:36-45). Because they slept, he felt even more alone as he was terrified and "sorrowful unto death" in the Garden of Olives.

Choosing: I will read the story about Jesus in the garden, his request to his friends and their response (Mt 26:36-45, Mk 14:32-41, Lk 22:39-46). I will recall a time when I have asked for emotional support and a time when I haven't done so, though I needed to.

Paying the Price: If I ask for help while I am already wounded, I may feel additional fear of laying my emotions open to someone else—who may lovingly accept me or, not knowing how to respond, add to my suffering.

Praying: Help me to accept my feelings and needs as you accepted yours.

To Consider

Shells of independence have many patterns. A person with a weak back may refuse to ask for help with something as simple as carrying packages. ("I can do it," or, "I don't want to be a bother to someone else.") Another person, recovering from surgery or an accident, may become angry and peevish at necessary caretakers.

If we resent the shattering of our image of independence, we may take it out on those trying to fill our needs. Worse, if we demand independence of ourselves, we will probably demand it of others. "Can't you just pull yourself together and get going?" If we feel powerless to help another, we may blame the person who has the need or difficulty.

We all need healing. Sometimes we may benefit from professional support to supply the process for this healing. Sometimes a good friend can help. How often have we heard, "I can get through this by myself," as we watched the speaker become tighter and tighter until we were afraid the effort would result in a heart attack, stroke, or breakdown?

Paul writes, "Bear one another's burdens" (Gal 6:2). Jesus tells us that the blind and the lame and the crippled come into the Community of God together (Lk 14:21). It is when we mutually recognize our needs and bring them to each other that we experience love, intimacy, care, and mutual support.

Many twelve-step programs and support groups
model this. So did the early Christian communities.
Filling each other's needs and permitting others to
fill ours is an entrance ticket into the Community of
God.

> *Choosing:* I will express some need, inner or
> outer, to the most trustworthy person I know
> among those available to me.

> *Paying the Price:* I may feel more alone in my
> need if the other does not understand or
> respond.

> *Praying:* Teach me to feel comfortable about
> being part of the interdependence of all creation.

To Consider

Would someone please form a support group for those of us who always try to speak properly, write correctly, and do things appropriately? I propose a name for the group: PIPs—Perfectly Imperfect Perfectionists. Meetings could begin with statements such as, "I am Ginny and I am a perfectionist. At a formal bridal shower last Sunday, I stood up before everyone only to realize that my knee-highs were sagging around my ankles." Or, "I am Jack and when I was sick last week and resting in my easy chair, I found myself trying to change the TV channel with the telephone buttons."

Members would describe something imperfectly done in the past week, laugh at themselves, and accept the laughter of others. Wouldn't that be freeing? Laughing is our best offense and defense. Affectionate laughter, our own and others, helps us to realize that we are loved not only in spite of our imperfections, but with them.

Choosing: I will laugh, or at least smile, at my mistakes today. If one of them is funny, I will tell someone else about it.

Paying the Price: That "someone else" may not smile.

Praying: Help me to recognize the imperfection of my perfectionism. Help me to laugh at myself.

TO CONSIDER

We wrap ourselves in the Perfect shell as a shield to stop the stings of criticism or the hostile thrusts of anger. Does it work? Of course not, as any perfectionist knows. But perfectionists are caught in feeling that even more rejection and criticism will target them if the shell opens up a bit.

In truth, who truly likes a perfect person (assuming there is one somewhere)? If someone even looks like a model for the rest of us, someone else is sure to look for flaws. When I was a teen-ager, I heard two of my classmates putting down a beautiful, popular girl who was also an exemplary student. Their criticism? "She's just too perfect."

All heroic and saintly people in history carry with them stories of criticism and rejection from their contemporaries. Even Mother Teresa, who exuded such loving service with inner freedom, received criticism.

We can only give up the effort to be perfect when we are able to accept the pain thrust by the knife of criticism.

Each crack we make in the shell of our perfectionism lets out some of the tension inside. Accepting ourselves with our imperfections also releases understanding and compassion toward others.

Choosing: The next time someone points out a fault or suggests a better way for me to do something, I will note my feelings. I will love those feelings whatever they may be. Am I tempted to defend some image of myself?

Paying the Price: I may have to surrender the self-image.

Praying: Help me to know that I do not need to be perfect in order to be wonderful.

TO CONSIDER

In support of perfectionism, some people quote Jesus' words in the Sermon on the Mount: "Be perfect, as *Abba* God is perfect" (Mt 5:48). Scripture scholars report that *perfect*, as we usually understand it, is a poor translation of the Hebrew word used in the phrase. Other nuanced words from the same Hebrew root *Shalom* mean "whole," "at peace with self and others," "mature." In the context of the passage, the word takes on the meaning of being maturely loving and compassionate as Jesus describes *Abba* in the preceding verses.

Jesus' idea of becoming *perfected* is that we grow in loving *Abba*, ourselves, and our neighbors as ourselves. Jesus grew in age, wisdom, and grace (Lk 2:50), and so do we. No one reaches the perfection of Christian love all at once. But we are a redeemed people, constantly being forgiven as we advance and fail along the way.

Full-fledged perfectionists are not the only ones who want to think of themselves as perfect. Many mini-perfectionists will say, in a tone of concession, "Well, I know I am not perfect." If someone else, however, mentions a particular way the speaker doesn't measure up to an expectation, we might watch and listen to the response.

Choosing: I will give myself understanding and compassion for each mistake I make.

Paying the Price: I will recognize that others may or may not give me the same.

Praying: Help me to love myself as you do.

TO CONSIDER

PIPs want to do each thing the "right" way. We try hard to get it right to prevent those critical knives from cutting us into pieces. At our worst, we demand "getting it right" from others. Of course, our way is the right way.

An antidote to perfectionism suggests that "if a thing is worth doing, it is worth doing badly." Scary words for those with the "impeccable" shells.

Excellent exercises for some kinds of perfectionists are as follows: leave one's bed unmade, jay-walk (carefully), wear mismatching shoes and don't explain why, come late to the meeting without giving an explanation. What may be vice for some can be virtue for others.

Exercises for other perfectionists: tune in to the inner voices that may be criticizing you; for example, "You didn't say that right"; "You shouldn't think that way"; "It's all your fault"; "You should be beyond feeling hurt about something like that"; "You ought to _____ (know more about foreign events, be a better listener, be a more clever conversationalist, be able to pray longer without distractions, never feel impatient with your children, do more without being so tired—and on and on and on)." Bringing these demanding voices out into the open dilutes their power.

Choosing: I will do one of the above exercises that will be a challenge for me.

Paying the Price: I will note and accept any feeling or thoughts that come from my inner voices and know that I do not have to follow anything they suggest.

Praying: Help me to let go of my continual striving.

TO CONSIDER

Scott receives lots of party invitations and is usually the central attraction at any gathering. His high spirits, wit, and willingness to play the comedian bring him notice and popularity. Humor seems to come naturally. Actually, it does. But it is only one part of Scott and, at one time, the only part he thought that anyone else wanted to know.

Scott had become like the proverbial clown who was "laughing on the outside, crying on the inside." His humor, a part of him, had become his whole image. The high spirit that adorned his shell got him some of the attention he craved, but not the affirmation and support which he needed for the rest of his person. Eventually, he felt the shell closing in on him. He began to drink heavily to suppress his sadness and loneliness.

Scott recognized that he needed to risk being accepted without his "funny face" by some person or persons. He felt afraid that most people would turn away if he revealed his inner self without the wit and humor. Deciding to find someone took courage. Fortunately, he took the risk. A friend listened to the pain and confusion he had carried for a long time. They spent many hours together, and Scott discovered other parts of himself that he had hidden. He found that they were acceptable and even lovable.

Scott can now choose to live openly in other parts of himself. Scott is in recovery for his alcoholism and is becoming freer to choose whether he wants to display his comic self or to live with his sadness in ways that will heal it.

Choosing: As I go through the day, how am I seeing myself in another person's eyes? What am I hoping the other will think about me? If I feel especially ready for a risk, I will ask what the other is thinking about me.

Paying the Price: I may feel hurt if I discover that someone has an image of me that I don't want—true or not.

Praying: Help me to know my hidden self better and to treasure each part of me as you do.

TO CONSIDER

To avoid being exiled from a group or treated with contempt, we might react to injustice by retreating to silence within our shell. For example, Emily tells a joke and its humor is based on a negative racial stereotype. A group at the office is passing around whispered, petty criticism of the woman who has just received a promotion. A rumor claims that an older person with years of service is about to be dismissed so that the pension due him in two years need not be paid. There is a buzz of suspicion in the neighborhood that a homeowner might sell her house to someone of a different racial or ethnic background, and some of the neighbors want to prevent the sale.

Of course we want to be part of our social group, office, or neighborhood. But standing—and perhaps alone—for our values is a risk. We fear being put down if we speak up. Reputation and possibly position are at stake. We may be side-lined and even bashed by the people we had thought were friends. Silence in the shell looks friendly. Maybe we will not even be noticed there, we think.

Speaking up is a challenge. Doing so without self-righteousness is an even bigger one. But silence chains the gospel-person within us.

Choosing: When does my following of Jesus conflict with other values in my life: for example, wanting to be liked, wanting advancement? What do I usually choose? Is some situation right now calling me to speak up?

Paying the Price: If I speak I may feel the suffering of being criticized, ignored, or ostracized.

Praying: Just One, help me to stand up for what is just, even if I have to stand alone.

$\mathscr{I}$mpression Management

What I call impression management is the art of designing, consciously or unconsciously, the impression we want to make on others. It is an attempt to influence and even control the way others think about us.

Madison Avenue leads the way as we go about making and distributing our self-images. Just by inhaling thousands of ads, we have become good students and practitioners of projecting what we want others to think. Unfortunately, faithfulness to the truth of a product isn't Madison Avenue's driving force. So we need to look at what motivates us as we present ourselves. We can reveal to others what is true, or we can project, instead, some impressive fluff. Living the truth will set us free. Fluff will choke us.

The Scottish poet Robert Burns describes a congregation watching a well-dressed lady as she walks up the aisle trying to impress her fellow church-goers with her stylishness. What catches people's eyes, however, is a louse that is slowly crawling up her hat. He writes:

> O wad some pow'r the giftie gie us
> To see oursel as others see us! ("To a Louse")

The irony of practicing impression management is that, like the lady in the poem, we have no control over what others think of us. It doesn't stop us, however, from trying to get it.

Wanting others to think well of us is natural. But energy spent on creating an image so that others can see us in a certain light is energy that binds rather than frees.

What is it that we would like others to think about us, including things that are true? We'll explore some possibilities in the following considerations.

To Consider

What kinds of things do we say to impress others? We may drop a name or the name of a group to "let people know" the kind of company we keep. We may plan something witty for a coming conversation or meeting. We may subtly or not so subtly mention some of our accomplishments. We may tell a story of how we told off an offending person to show that we are "not to be messed with." We may compliment another just to get an appreciative response. We may be silent—out of fear that what we say will negatively impress.

None of the above would put us in competition for Culprit of the Year. When people like, admire, or respect us, it adds warmth and pleasure to our lives. It can encourage the best in us and nourish friendships.

We can become more free, however, by letting go of the subtle effort to manipulate others into liking or appreciating us through what we say. Besides, we cannot do it. Others see us through the lens of their own personality glasses. We already know that things we have said are often heard differently than we intend them. Mostly, though, we lose our freedom to grow in the confidence to be just who we are.

Of course, just being ourselves doesn't mean that we blurt out everything that comes to mind. We want to treat the "selves" of others in the way we want them to treat us—with respect for them and their feelings. Becoming more free requires balance between being honest and still considering the effect of our words on others.

Choosing: I will ask myself if I ever try to control, by what I say, how another thinks of me. If so, I will accept this in myself with love and ask for the power of the Spirit to grow in freedom.

Paying the Price: Giving up verbal impression management may result in feeling afraid that no one will like my true self.

Praying: Jesus, Word of God, let my words speak only the truth in humility and love.

To Consider

Explaining ourselves is another form of impression management. After all, we don't want people to get the wrong impression of us. So we describe incidents in such ways as, "There was a character on *Days of Our Lives* who said—now, I seldom watch soap operas—but, he said. . . ."

Or, how about, "I'm sorry I'm late, I'm hardly ever late, and what happened was. . . ."

Or, "I didn't get to the meeting, but. . . ."

It's pretty harmless stuff, yet we feel an underlying tension in trying to maintain a particular self-image that always needs defending.

We may have all kinds of things which we want others to believe about us: that we are effective, loyal, hard-working, accurate with details, seldom or never afraid, uncomplaining, knowledgeable of the facts, able to handle our feelings and situations by ourselves, seldom angry, not easily taken advantage of or fooled. The self-images may be true, not true, or sometimes true. But we explain ourselves to defend the impression we want to give.

Aren't we just being human in doing so? Of course. Are we bad people for doing this? Of course not. Will we become more free if we can let go of defending our images? Absolutely.

Choosing: I will listen to myself or ask someone to listen to me and note any times that I unnecessarily explain myself. I will ask myself: What self-images am I grasping?

Paying the Price: When I don't explain, the other may, indeed, make a wrong judgment about me.

Praying: Loving One, I know I am loved by you no matter what others may think of me.

To Consider

Impression management may take the form of silence, or of speaking very little. An old saying tells us to "Keep quiet and let people think you are stupid rather than open your mouth and let them know it for sure." Sad advice.

We can hold back on our words, our thoughts, and our opinions, attempting to look wise or to avoid looking foolish. We may fear reporting something we know or think because we are afraid of criticism or disagreement, or worse, of being ignored.

We constantly make judgments about when to speak and when to be silent. Are any of these decisions based on fear? Are we free enough to speak our thoughts honestly? We may be surprised to see how they take flight for good. Yet, we cannot know for sure. That is why speaking up unites us with a risk-taking God.

Choosing: I will be aware of my reasons for keeping silent and ask myself if they are wise or if they are binding me.

Paying the Price: We may feel hurt when some of our words are discounted or misunderstood.

Praying: Give me wisdom to know when to speak and when to be silent.

TO CONSIDER

Following the lead of Madison Avenue, we may dress-to-impress. We may dress up to make an impression, dress down for effect, or try to blend in so as not to be noticed. We may even dress outrageously off-style to make visual statements about our beliefs, connections, life-models, or rebellion against the *status quo*. It is all the same—if, by doing so, we are trying to sell others on the way we want them to think of us.

Naturally, we want to look attractive to others. Each of us has styles of dressing that genuinely express our personalities. The Beautiful Mystery is reflected in earth's beauty—and in ours. The way we dress can be a cooperation in the beauty and creativity of God. Dressing-to-express is different from dressing-to-impress.

We dress-to-impress when we deliberately give an image of something we are not. Perhaps we want others to consider us wealthier than we are, or as living a simpler lifestyle than we are. We might dress to give the impression that we belong to the young and adventuresome set, or the motorcycle gang, or the earth movement—because we want someone's acceptance.

Choosing: The next time I dress or change my clothes, I will ask if I am dressing to project an image that is a strain to maintain. If so, I will laugh at myself, being aware that I cannot control anyone else's opinion. I will ask myself if I can let go of anything regarding dress so as to have less luggage to enter into God's freedom.

Paying the Price: Those with superficial values may judge me. I may feel some hurt if I am left out or wrongly judged.

Praying: Creative Mystery, thank you for allowing me to share in your creativity as I express myself in the clothes I wear.

TO CONSIDER

Jesus' admonition about clothing is the following:
Why be anxious about clothing?
Learn a lesson from the way the wildflowers grow.
They don't work; they don't spin.
Yet I tell you, not even Solomon in full splendor
   was arrayed like one of these.
If God can clothe in such splendor the grasses
   of the field,
which bloom today and are thrown on to the
   fire tomorrow,
won't God do so much more for you—you who
   have so little faith? (Mt 6:28-30).

Jesus wants to free us with this statement. Do not worry about clothes or even the beauty of clothes! The freedom could be extended to include not being anxious about how we are seen or judged by others because of what we wear.

Besides, we cannot control what interpretation, what judgments others might make because of our clothing. A fashionably dressed person may be admired by one, seen as uppity by another, and not be noticed by a third. How often have we stereotyped someone who dressed in a strange or displeasing way and then found a person underneath that we came to appreciate or even love!

To become free of dressing-to-impress, we might ask: Am I dressing as my genuine self (or a genuine part of myself) within the circumstances? Am I striving for an impression that will imprison me if I must continually try to live up to it? Are my clothes taking on undue importance in my life? Does buying clothing send me into debt? Do I devote a disproportionate amount of time to shopping?

Choosing: I will consider whether my clothing is interfering in any way with my freedom.

Paying the Price: I may need to give up dressing-to-impress or lower my emphasis on shopping and clothing.

Praying: Thank you for the clothing I have. Help me use it freely and creatively.

$\mathcal{H}$ands off the Wheel

Before I begin a period of centering prayer, which invites me to let go of everything except my awareness of the present moment, I instruct the Manager of the Universe: "You are now in charge of everything for the next twenty minutes. I will try to let go of my control and trust you to run everything without me. Okay?" (Do I hear a small, cosmic chortle?) During this time, however, I take back my "controls," catch myself in the process, and return to the centering—over and over again.

If you want to check some of the ways you, along with most of us, try to control others, the world around you, or yourself, jot down your distractions when you are praying or meditating. Or, what you are thinking while driving a car or doing the laundry? How many thoughts have to do with planning? With what you want to say to someone or how to say it? With what you wish you would have replied to someone yesterday? Do any of them have to do with imagining what you could say

79

to "make him realize . . ."? With day-dreaming ways to get her to change her way of thinking or acting?

We attempt to control in order to protect the outside of the shell even when we are retreating inside of it. We design ways to keep others from challenging our view of life, or to get them to fill our needs, or to secure assurances that what they will say and do will keep us feeling comfortable—emotionally or physically. By controlling others, we not only imprison ourselves, but we put another shell around them—in addition to the one they already have. Then we bump shells rather than enjoy genuine relationships.

In healthy adult relationships, persons tell each other what they need, what they want, and, if they are doing something together, how they each want to do it. Then they work out ways so that each one's desires can be fulfilled as much as possible. They compromise when their needs clash. In unhealthy relationships, however, persons try to get what they want by manipulating or controlling the other. Power struggles, overt and subtle, result. Learning not to control—or be controlled—is a necessary part of the curriculum for living freely.

Jesus calls us to a love of self that frees us and to a love of others that frees them.

> When Christ freed us, we were meant to remain free. Stand firm, and do not submit to slavery a second time! (Gal 5:1).

We might extend this command: Do not try to enslave anyone else either.

Controlling or Choosing?

Exercising control is different from making choices. We usually spin into controlling behavior to avoid the suffering which is inevitable in our lives. We may control and suppress our real selves to avoid criticism or rejection. We may try to control others to get something we want or need. We may try to control nature, our material world, to make ourselves financially secure. We may even fool ourselves into thinking we can control, by bargaining, the One-Who-Holds-All-Power.

Our wheels of control roll with many spokes. One of them presses down our emotions so that we won't suffer the erupting sadness, anger, or fear that invades us in response to loss, insult, or pain. Sometimes we keep these feelings pressed down under alcohol, overwork, shopping, or unhealthy relationships. While this behavior is not hard to understand, it only leads us deeper into our shells where further choices become severely limited. We cramp, even suffocate, our experience of life.

Another spoke attempts to control other people since their choices contribute to our own happiness or suffering. Others may give us love or rejection, understanding or misunderstanding, protection or abandonment, kindness or abuse, praise or criticism. Having experienced some share of each, we want to control which ones we will receive again. We are tempted to manipulate or intimidate.

One way to "force" others to do what we want is to provide some discomfort if they don't. We may simply be fishing for compliments and then begin pouting if they don't come. Or we may become hypochondriacs, using illness to get others to pay attention and conform to our wishes. The punishment for failing to do what the controller wants might be turning a shoulder, refusing to speak, withholding signs of love, or walking out on a relationship. In the business, academic, and health-care worlds, it may be firing or withholding a deserved promotion, refusing salary increases, or eliminating perks. In the religious and social world, it may be smudging someone's reputation, "Now, she's a good person, but. . . ."

A third spoke attempts an unhealthy control of circumstances. While it is appropriate to use caution to stay out of danger, it becomes detrimental to avoid all risks—from traffic, from travel, from meeting someone new or someone whose ideas may threaten ours. We easily become isolated.

Still another spoke tries to control the material world. At its worst, the controlling person may break laws to get more money—by burglary, inflating insurance claims, or inside trading in the stock market. He may destroy the environment to make the corporation more lucrative. She may put others at risk by deciding to use unsafe materials to cut costs and increase profit.

He might spend every minute focused on work or investments. She might be stingy with family or friends or be unwilling to share with those less fortunate as she attempts to control future security.

Is Control Effective?

Does control work? Often it does for a while—not only for individuals, but also for religious or ethnic groups and nations, as well as for racial and gender groups. Does it lead to some short-term rewards for the controlling one? Frequently. Does it lead to the freedom, love, peace, or unity that is the Community of God? Never.

When we bind another, we bind ourselves with the same cords.

When we use our freedom to twist others into giving us what seems good to our egos, to bend others to live in a way that supports us, to avoid the suffering that comes into our lives, we eventually roll into quicksand of loneliness, depression, returned hostility, bitterness, and even despair. We sink farther down with each attempt to struggle out.

Whenever we try to take away the freedom of others, we are following the temptation of Adam and Eve; we, too, want to be as gods—safe, powerful, and in control (Gn 3:5). According to Jesus, however, these values are un-godly. Our Ultimate Risk-Taker does not clutch security, power, or control.

To enter into new life and freedom, we must begin walking, vulnerably, a labyrinthine way. At each turn in the maze, we will meet the emotions from which we were trying to run, or come face to face with the difficulties that we are avoiding in our relationships, or recognize that much of our world is out of our control. What do we do then?

If we choose to follow Jesus' example, we will let ourselves feel the hurt, sadness, anger, fear, or powerlessness called up by these encounters. For, among all the great spiritual leaders, Jesus' unique Way is his walk into loneliness, betrayal, physical pain, criticism, abandonment, misunderstanding, the jealousy of others, and condemnation even to death. Jesus shows us that it is the walk *through* the suffering, not the avoidance of it, that leads to new life. Jesus says, "Come, follow me" (Mt 10:38).

It is partly our insufficient belief in the good news that tempts us to control. Instead of trusting ourselves to the palm of the Open Hand, we try to establish our own safety. But we do not have a safe leader, one who protects us from suffering. Rather, we have one who has experienced every kind of suffering and walks through it with us.

The following considerations are examples of day-to-day ways we try to control others to prevent our own suffering. Acknowledging them is the first step to taking our hands off the wheel—a scary thing to do unless we believe in another Hand which will hold us on course.

To Consider

Kim worries that her sister Sarah is on a slippery slope. She notices Sarah picking up books on spirituality that don't come out of their common church background. She realizes that Sarah occasionally goes to groups that talk about past-life experiences, auras, and the healing power of crystals. Sarah occasionally questions traditional beliefs that she and Kim have always held.

Kim wants her sister back in agreement with her. So she makes derogatory remarks to Sarah about her "simplistic thinking," or "paganism." She hurls the label "New Age" at her as if it were the ultimate accusation. Sarah, in turn, tosses "narrow-minded" or "intellectually stuck" at Kim. "Ultra-conservative" is her supreme insult.

Labeling and insulting are means of control. Kim thinks they will control Sarah's explorations beyond what she considers her own boundaries of belief. Sarah thinks she will control Kim's judgments. Both want to imprison the other for different reasons.

Will either change? Probably not. If they continue in this way, their relationship will probably stagnate and they will drift apart. When anyone controls, a loving relationship cannot grow.

Choosing: I will ask myself the following questions: When do I try to control another by labeling instead of listening—even if I disagree? Do I try to control anyone by derogatory remarks, suggesting she will no longer be acceptable to me if she disagrees with me, or does something of which I disapprove? When do I thus imprison another and pull a stronger shell around myself?

Paying the Price: Accepting my fear. Am I ready to expose my inner self by asking for discussion and trying to understand the other, even if I disagree?

Praying: You-Who-Are-One, and You-Who-Express-Yourself-in-Diversity, help me to be open to others who think differently than I do.

To Consider

Angie knows how everyone else should live and how things ought to be done, and she is not afraid to let anyone know it. "It's for his own good!" she tells anyone who has the courage to confront her behavior. For whose good? Recipients of her advice don't find it to theirs.

Angie wants to be sure everything is under control—her control. If someone does not follow her commands, you can find her muttering to herself or to anyone within listening distance.

Her shell is a hard one to pry open. She will brook no discussion of her orders. She will imprison you in them if you let her. She will try to make life hellish if you don't.

Running from her is an option. Unfortunately, Angie does not have many friends.

Choosing: I will ask myself: Are there any subtle or overt ways I try to tell others what they "should" do and how to do it? Is there a bossy part of me, maybe less obvious than Angie's, that wants to enclose others in my instruction boxes? What is it that I fear?

Paying the Price: If I let go, I may have to take the consequences if something I fear actually happens.

Praying: You-Who-Create-Uniqueness-and-Diversity, help me to let others be who they are and do things the way they choose.

TO CONSIDER

Brian is large and strong and uses his body to intimidate. He is a boss who lets it be known that there will be consequences for anyone stepping out of his line of thinking or ways of doing. He will stare you down with jutted jaw. Although physical punishment may be implied, Brian can mete out other kinds also. He will report you to the manager, deprive you of your parking space, send his dog to relieve itself on your lawn, turn up his stereo to blast your eardrums, ignore your next legitimate request—all to let you know you have not pleased him. You may have made an honest suggestion, disagreed with him, done your job your own way, or not paid him what he considers his due recognition. He will get even. Things must go the way he wants them to go.

Brian is not free and he will try to imprison you. Standing up to him, if you can, is an option. So is staying out of his way.

Choosing: Do I ever try to control another by implying that negative consequences will follow if things are not done my way?

Paying the Price: I must accept the consequences of others doing things their way.

Praying: Help me to let others make their own decisions.

To Consider

Story 1: Mrs. L., an elderly woman in our parish, asked me to stop by her home. She and her sister had lived together on the first floor of a two-family house, which they owned. Her sister had died a few months ago. She was understandably grieving and lonely.

Mrs. L. wanted to talk to me about the woman who had rented the upstairs a month ago. She was feeling hurt and rejected by the renter who was only minimally polite to her and usually cut off any attempts at social conversation. She was angry and wanted me to support her anger.

"I even gave her the apartment at a reduced rent, thinking that she would be companionable," she told me.

"Did you tell her this?" I asked.

"No, I just thought that, since I let her stay for less money, she should be more friendly to me."

Story 2: Hannah wants others at work to be her friends, remember her birthday, show an interest in what she is doing outside her workplace. Fine. She can ask for these things by initiating an agreement with her co-workers to celebrate everyone's birthday, or inviting someone to go to a movie or out to dinner as a way of courting a friendship, or asking someone to listen to her at break about a problem at home. Instead, she begins lavishing presents on others, looking for ways to help them complete their tasks, staying overtime for others, or working on the days that everyone wants to be off. She doesn't tell her co-workers that she expects friendship, presents, and the interest of others in return. By her favors, she is trying to manipulate them into giving her what she wants. When it doesn't work, we will hear an angry Hannah complaining about all she has done for others and how little they appreciate it.

Choosing: I ask myself: Do I ever give or do things for another only with the expectation of return (other than a thank-you)?

Paying the Price: If I am manipulating others, trying to get what I want without asking for it, I need to reconsider my behavior.

Praying: I need your courage to be open and honest with myself and others.

To Consider

"He is always against me no matter what I say."

"She is so selfish."

"He just wants to upset me."

"You think you are superior to me."

"Pushy broad! She is after my position."

Mark, occasionally called "The Paranoid" behind his back, tries to control others by insinuating their motives (always negative ones, of course) whenever they refuse to agree with him or do things his way. It is another version of name-calling and labeling done in order to take power and to avoid talking about an issue. If Mark is in authority, he may get his way. But people will also choose to stay out of his way. Being controlled or being insulted is not a good set of choices.

Choosing: I will ask myself if I ever attribute motives to people who do not do what I want them to do, act as I want them to act, say what I want them to say. What am I trying to avoid by my negativity? Is one of my self-images threatened?

Paying the Price: Feeling the fear of having my self-images challenged.

Praying: Merciful One, help me not to judge the motives of others.

TO CONSIDER

Maureen is sick again. Predictably. You can count on some display of illness if she does not get her way. Sometimes, when experiencing disagreement with someone, she just acts fragile and puts on a "Now-don't-hurt-me" face. If necessary, she will call up tears. She tries to control by laying guilt ("I am weak and you have hurt me") on those around her who do not say or do what she wants.

Maureen suffers, as most of us do at times, when she doesn't get what she wants. But Maureen tries to make the other person suffer instead, and manipulates to regain control.

Tanya also uses her emotions to control others. If a supervisor or family member points out a mistake she has made, or brings up anything that might be improved in her behavior, her eyes fill with tears. Her message is clear: "Back off or you are responsible for devastating me." Some people do stay away, and all of Tanya's relationships are strained.

Eric, too, uses a display of emotions to control. Just disagree or suggest that anything he has done is less than perfect and you have slid the lid off a volcano. Intimidation is his game of control. Prepare for the blow-up.

Choosing: Do I ever try to make others feel guilty when they are not doing what I want? Do I ever show anger, outwardly or subtly, when I am challenged by others?

Paying the Price: I may need to accept disagreement, questions, or challenges about the way I do things.

Praying: Help me to neither control nor be controlled.

To Consider

Gayle gets up from the table, leaves the room, and lets the door slam ever so slightly behind her. Those remaining at the table get her message. Gayle is angry about something that was said. The others may or may not know what she found offensive. Later, when someone in the group approaches her, she tosses her head and walks on. When someone else asks her what she is angry about, she throws this answer back at them with a set jaw and flashing eyes:

"Me? Angry? I don't get angry."

If someone mentions her behavior, she replies, "I was finished eating and wanted to do something else. Can I help it if the door slammed behind me?"

Not free to accept and acknowledge her anger, and afraid of having anyone question her objections to what was said or done, Gayle tries to punish the group into saying only what she wants to hear in the future.

Others need a healthy courage to keep confronting her and not be controlled by her passive-aggressive behavior, by the way she aggresses them while disclaiming her intentions to do so.

·

Choosing: Do I ever give others the silent treatment? Do I ever subtly punish another rather than speak of what is bothering me? If I am not sure, I will ask someone else who knows me well.

Paying the Price: Examining oneself takes time and courage. Asking another takes even more courage.

Praying: Help me to treat others as Jesus treated them.

TO CONSIDER

The worst kind of PIP (Perfectly Imperfect Perfectionist) is one who tries to make others perfect. Perfectionists often have hidden (sometimes repressed) or explosive anger which they feel to be dangerous. If the world and others could just be perfect, that anger would not be triggered. Depression or explosions could be averted. So PIPs try to change others and the way they do things to avoid their own angry feelings.

Some perfectionists will say there is a *right* and a *wrong* way of doing anything. They are eager, sometimes with genuinely good intentions, to explain the *right* one. They may criticize others, what they do and how they do it. They can point out what the other *should* have done and how. As they try to improve others, they can make them quite angry— in their own attempts to avoid anger.

Choosing: 1) I will note an imperfection of someone I love and graciously accept it as I remember one of my own quirks with the same acceptance; and 2) I will refrain from showing someone else a "better" way, unless that person asks for one.

Paying the Price: 1) I have to give up trying to change the other and accept my own anger; and 2) I may experience the astonishment of recognizing that someone else's way may be better than mine.

Praying: Help me to laugh at the imperfections of the world as I laugh at myself.

$\mathcal{O}$ther Entrances
to Freedom

The Providential Mystery has never promised that all will go well for us on earth. Jesus never declared that anything we do will exempt us from the suffering which mysteriously invades life. No religion or science has ever offered a reasonable explanation for why all living beings suffer. Neither does Jesus. He does, however, show us how to meet unavoidable physical and emotional pain and move through it to a renewed life.

This chapter considers some of the daily ways in which, consciously or unconsciously, we choose to turn our backs when Jesus says, "Come, follow me." We shrink away as he walks toward Jerusalem to be betrayed, abandoned, scourged, crowned with thorns, and nailed on a cross for all to see. Understandably, like Peter and most of the disciples, we shudder and run to hide in the inside of our shells. Our efforts to avoid suffering, however, cause us greater misery and inhibit our freedom.

If we choose to follow Jesus, we will enter into unknown places, and each entrance will require the suffering of leaving something behind. Some of the entrances are as follows:

- a tunnel where we must leave our ambition for status behind so that we can stoop low enough to crawl through;

- a low, limbo-dance rod which forces us to discard unnecessary material goods so that we can slip under it;

- a sliding door where we close behind us our pursuit of pleasure to take up our search for what will open us to joy;

- a narrow gate that we cannot enter when we are holding on to baggage stuffed with past hurts.

The Tunnel: Letting Go of Striving for Status or Recognition

In the opening of the classic stage play *The Fantastics*, a lovely, teen-aged girl is looking into the moonlight and singing to the heavens about the possibilities her life might hold. She ends with an intense plea, "And, please, don't let me be ordinary."

In each of the four times I have seen this musical, the audience responds to her words with an affectionate sigh/laugh of understanding. It is as if each of us remembers a youthful desire to be special in some way: tossing in the winning basket at a championship game, engaging in the perfect and lasting romance, starring in a rock concert, becoming an astronaut, addressing the U.S. Senate on the environment, raising the perfect, loving family, or discovering the cure for leukemia. When I entered my religious community at eighteen, I was confident that I could learn to be as holy as St. Thérèse of Lisieux in just two or three years.

We must dream our dreams and pursue them. We need and want to use all of our gifts and more toward making our dreams come true. But when do we reach the time when the ambition is no longer a joyful pursuit but a pressure which we put on ourselves? When do we begin to measure our value and our success by our achievements, position, or possessions rather than by God's love? When do our ambitions become compulsive instead of relaxed expressions of the gifts we have to give?

The sigh of the audiences at *The Fantastics* carries the pathos that comes from understanding the difference between the wonderful dreams of the young girl and the lived reality that most of us spend our lives in Plan B . . . or C . . . or ? The audience also seems to understand that moving from one to the other may be a gentle slide or a rocky avalanche. Either way, life usually brings us to the reality of our everyday ordinariness, as the play reflects.

When we release ourselves from the pressure of our ambitions, we walk out into a new land of freedom. We leap with joy, knowing that ordinary is not only okay, it is—or can be—holy. We can then separate our achievements from who we are, our needs from our wants, and give up trying to save the world. We are able to be realistic about what we can truly accomplish within the acre or yard of our influence. When we become free of the stress of attaining or maintaining status, we recognize, peacefully, both our gifts and our limitations. We can forget trying to project ourselves as always being right, special, or competent. We can be ordinary human beings doing what we are able to do and letting go of the rest. We become free to love, to be more intimate. We become free to live as an unencumbered pearl in the Reign of God.

Although we don't look back on Jesus as ordinary, most of his contemporaries did. Nazareth? A woodworker's son? One who had to grow—as we do—in age, wisdom, and grace? An itinerant preacher? One who followed the rituals of his religion and asked to be baptized? A common man put to death as a common criminal? Yet, in his ordinariness, Jesus seems to be the freest human being who ever lived.

The Limbo Rod: Leaving Unnecessary Possessions Behind

Participants begin the limbo by dancing and, in rhythm with the music, slipping back and forth under a rod held parallel to the ground. As they dance, the rod is set lower and lower. The most skilled of the dancers continue to slip gracefully under the rod and return for each lower setting. When the rod is set a few inches from the ground, only the lightest and most limber of dancers can bend and slide under. This is another metaphor, perhaps, for Jesus' caution that it is difficult for those who have many possessions to enter the Reign of freedom.

A *Business Week* poll listed inventions Americans said that they couldn't live without. Among them were the automobile, light bulb, telephone, television, aspirin, microwave oven, blow-dryer, and PC. What a great list for distinguishing between what we can't live without and what we don't want to live without, between our needs and our desires! If we asked poor or indigenous people from developing countries for such a list, what would they put on it?

Do we possess, or are we possessed by, our possessions?

Is material poverty a good? Are we more holy without material things? The answers are complex. Although Jesus told the person who wanted to be perfect to "sell everything you own and give the money to those poorer than you . . . then come and follow me" (Lk 18:22), neither the Jewish nor the Christian scriptures praises poverty in itself. If poverty were good, we would do better to help our brothers and sisters remain in their neediness than to support their emergence from it.

Yet, Francis of Assisi *loved* being poor. He loved the freedom he felt when he gave away all his possessions. He no longer had to spend time building, maintaining, or defending anything. He preferred trusting in the goodness of other people as he begged for daily necessities rather than spending his days earning and building his fortune. He was free to preach, to pray, to enjoy the earth.

Is this kind of freedom of possessions for most of us? Hardly! But we do love Francis because he touches truth that we know in the core of ourselves. He shows us what Madison Avenue does not want us to discover: that while our possessions may give us comfort, convenience, or pleasure, they do not give us freedom and the "peace that the world cannot give."

While poverty is not a good in itself, neither is wealth. Unfortunately we constrict ourselves and even our relationships more tightly when we focus on financial security and acquiring and maintaining "things."

Becoming free means that we consider how we feel about our possessions. We ask ourselves: What are my needs? Can I separate them from my wants? Am I willing to share anything that goes beyond my needs? Am I willing to share even in my neediness?

Do I put myself under stress to acquire more than I need? Does shopping and cleaning limit my time with loved ones? Does a second TV keep me and my partner from compromising on what we want to watch and from enjoying programs together? Does my garage-door opener keep me from daily contact with my neighbors?

Do I realize, if I am a U.S. citizen, that I live in the upper five percent of the world's wealthy no matter how simply I am living?

Jesus warned that rich people have difficulty in entering the kindom, but he did not condemn wealth. Rather, the passage points out how hard it is to hold our possessions lightly and let them go when we are called to do so. They too easily block our passage into freedom.

You cannot serve two bosses, Jesus explains: "You will either hate one and love the other, or be attentive to one and despise the other" (Mt 6:24). You cannot work for your freedom and for wealth at the same time.

It is helpful to ask ourselves: What would I find hardest to share? to give away? to live without?

The Door: Is the "Good Life" All That Good?

Critics of culture point out that movies and TV now provide so many explicitly sexual scenes that casual sex appears to be normal. For decades, movies and TV shows have presented all kinds of pleasure, particularly sexual pleasure, as the road to happiness. Perhaps these messages are reacting to an almost puritanical attitude toward sexual pleasure in the 1930s, '40s, and '50s. But both views evade the truth that the Uniting Mystery offers us the gift of sexuality to be enjoyed— within responsible freedom. Perhaps no other gift in life has given so much joy-filled pleasure or caused so much unhappiness, struggle, and disaster. Sexual choices can free us or chain us.

Advertising is important to our capitalist economy. Many ads are artistic, sophisticated, or humorous.

Some even offer a few positive values. Yet millions of advertisements show pursuing pleasure and avoiding pain as our daily goal. None of us is immune to the messages. Corporations pay millions for a spot on Superbowl Sunday despite consumers' protests that ads don't affect them. Advertisers know better.

Ironically, it is sometimes a good film that best shows us the emptiness of the messages portrayed in other films and the media. Such is Fellini's Italian classic *La Dolce Vita*, which presents a man spending seven nights in Rome pursuing a different pleasure each night. He finishes the week mired in emptiness. The Academy Award winning film *American Beauty* also shows the pursuit of wealth, status, and sexual pleasure as leading only to boredom, not the happiness they promise. They could be called morality plays, although the conclusions they present are the result of life experiences rather than religious teachings.

Entering the Reign of God certainly does not mean leaving all pleasure behind. It means receiving all of God's gifts with respect and love and not running after pleasure in a mistaken race for happiness.

The Narrow Gate: The Challenge of Forgiving Love

Jesus tells us that others will identify us as his followers if they see that we love one another. It is Jesus' forgiveness of others that offers us the most difficult challenge to this love. Like him we are to repair the breaches of the heart and to bridge the abysses that divide us from ourselves and one another. When someone assaults us, verbally or physically, we want to wield similar weapons in return. We are emotionally wired to want to even the score. It seems like justice. But that is just an illusion. Ultimately, revenge will not bring about justice. It will spread evil and create more division. Knowing this, our Teacher counters with, "Do not return evil for evil." Following a Jesus who forgave his enemies is our great challenge.

Jesus calls us even further than forgiveness, to the radical act of doing good to our enemies rather than hurting them. But he never said that we could not defend ourselves, or put up a shield to stop someone from hurling a knife or an insult at us. Our challenge says, "Don't return the thrust or put-down." It is different to stand firm and say, "No more of this" than it is to aggress the other. Returning evil just spawns more of it—as we can see in the killing among ethnic or religious groups, the breaking down of families, and the destruction of working relationships and friendships. Only refusing to return the evil slows or stops its growth. Revenge takes us into a darkened country; forgiveness takes us into the radiance of the Light of the World, the Community of God.

Chosen anger hardens a heart into a jagged rock. Its dryness absorbs our energy and focus. Eventually, it may damage our health. For our own sake, we must begin a process of forgiveness. One part of that process is accepting the full feelings of the pain inflicted by the other. Another is asking for the power of the Spirit to forgive. Another may be talking with someone who can support this journey to freedom.

Deep hurts require time to heal. We may will to forgive, yet not be free of feeling the hurt and anger. Forgiveness, in the least, means that we resolve not to wish or do any harm to the other. That is a decision. At the most, it means praying for the good of the other. That is also a decision. Feeling may or may not follow. Perhaps Jesus asked *Abba* to forgive his enemies (Lk 23:34) because, at that moment, he was not humanly able to *feel* forgiveness himself.

In the following considerations, we look at some of the choices we need to make—and the ones we need to avoid—if we want to fit through the entrances to the Community of God.

To Consider

When I left my orange tabby cat in the temporary care of a friend, I began my written instructions, "If you want to make friends with him, he likes to be noticed, talked to, petted, and praised."

Then I thought, Don't we all!

We* feel good when someone notices us in a crowd and comes over to say hello. We can be more motivated by someone's recognition and praise than by any other reward. When we show and receive appreciation, we fill each other's human need to feel positively connected. We become part of building a wholesome community.

Showing appreciation and praising another requires inner freedom, especially if we are to do it without fawning, flattering, or passing off polite, expected phrases. We need to be able to let go of self-images and impression-management to focus on another's goodness, gifts, or accomplishments. We need to let go of any feelings of competition with the person, or of any comparisons in which we may feel ourselves inadequate.

Choosing: I will notice how many times today I give sincere appreciation, praise, or compliments to another.

Paying the Price: Letting go of whatever keeps me from verbalizing my appreciation.

Praying: Make me aware that recognizing someone else's value never diminishes my own.

To Consider

Appreciation has a cousin, an inflated sort of fellow called Status. Status also motivates, but unlike Appreciation, Status wants to stand *above* others, to be admired and deferred to, to be granted privileges.

Working for Status can be exhilarating at first. It can lead to measurable success such as a promotion, inclusion in some group, power over others' lives, or recognition for one's specialness or creativity. But Status can also devastate his followers. Growing more shells seems to be a requisite for the preservation of Status. Overwork for promotion or power so often weakens and destroys relationships. Specialness deplores being viewed as part of the common folk. Status isolates.

To enter the Community of God, followers of Status have to let go of many thick layers of pretense and defense. They have to puncture their inflated feelings of entitlement before they can bend low enough to make their way through the tunnel that leads to freedom.

Choosing: I will be clear about my goals in my work and social life. Am I giving and receiving appreciation? Or am I climbing a ladder, stepping on others' hands, to reach some reward of status? I will be aware of any small choices I make today.

Paying the Price: Not looking for the so-called rewards of status: entitlement, preference, privileges.

Praying: Help me to be with others as a treasured person among other treasured persons.

TO CONSIDER

Leisure and Pleasure are wonderful companions and playmates. They give us relaxation, stimulation, energy, and joy. Leisure is essential for prayer and friendships; Pleasure is a gift that enhances our lives. Together, they can free us to be open to the Gracious Beauty of Life and heighten our ability to express love.

Some of us, however, are wary about leisure and afraid of pleasure. Warnings abound:

"You'll become lazy."

"You'll grow fat."

"You have no discipline."

"You're wasting time just sitting there dreaming."

"Don't be so self-centered, so self-indulgent."

The warnings are not without a ring of truth. For, while some can be afraid of spending time with Leisure and Pleasure, others dance with them so long that they disturb other important values in their lives. Both extremes diminish balance and freedom.

We can relax and enjoy the pleasures of life or become addicted to them: food, drink, sex, comfort, and distraction. Those who take leisure and pleasure to excess are usually aware of it. Those who are reluctant to take time off or to do something they enjoy for themselves, spiritually or physically, are often blind to their lack of freedom.

Our Generous Mystery wants us to enjoy our lives and to be free.

Choosing: I will ask myself: Am I out of balance in that I give myself too little leisure and pleasure, or too much? Or am I free and balanced in this regard?

Paying the Price: If I am not in balance, I may need to make difficult changes.

Praying: Thank you for your gifts of time and pleasure! I want to enjoy them and use them well.

To Consider

We need *stuff* to live: food, clothing, a place to sleep and feel safe, means of travel, money for education and health care. We name these as necessities. If you are reading this book, chances are that you have all or most of the above.

Over two-thirds of the persons on this earth lack one or more of these basics. They are parents, sons and daughters, grandparents, brothers and sisters just like us. Each of them is an individual with all of the same desires that we have for ourselves and our families.

Should we feel guilty about what we have? No! We should feel sad for those with less, but not guilty; angry at the injustice of economic systems the continually enrich some while impoverishing others, but not guilty. Guilt of this kind only depletes our energy to do anything positive.

Our freedom is connected with the freedom of all of our brothers and sisters. At some point in our journey of freedom, we understand this. Then we ask, "But what can I do?"

We can all choose to do several things to free ourselves and others:

- Know that each person is our brother or sister, and choose awareness and compassion rather than rationalizing judgments that give us an excuse for putting them out of mind, e.g., "But money goes farther in their country," or "They aren't suffering because they've never had these things," or "They are just lazy and haven't worked as hard as we have." Who could say these things directly to a mother and father whose child is dying from malnutrition or a curable illness like diarrhea?

- Share what we can of our money, *stuff*, or time with those we can help personally or through organizations. What *stuff* would make us freer if we gave it away?

- Read and listen to information on economic monopolies and speak up when full-time workers—in our country or any other—are not paid a *living* wage. Use our political freedom to protest, to raise consciousness of people we know, and to write to officials.

Choosing: I will do *something* to contribute to a redistribution of the resources of our earth. What do I possess that restricts my freedom?

Paying the Price: Giving up some of my time and/or my *stuff*. Refraining from judgments, recognizing my limited knowledge of most situations.

Praying: Everyone in the world is my brother or sister. Help them also to be free.

To Consider

Ignatius of Loyola lived as a soldier, serving the king of Spain in the sixteenth century. In his free time, he pursued women, engaged in duels, and enjoyed the pleasures and status that came with spending time at the royal court. While recuperating from a serious leg wound caused by a cannon ball, he had extensive time on his hands and could do little except read. He had wanted some romance stories but few books were available. He spent a great deal of time daydreaming of the pleasures of the court and of the women he knew. In desperate boredom, he picked up two books that were in the castle: the Bible and a book on the lives of the saints.

Over the months, he noticed that while his daydreams left him restless and unsatisfied, the gospels and the lives of the saints uplifted and freed him. He was intrigued. That difference was so powerful that, after his healing, he chose to abandon his soldiering career in order to preach and teach the Good News. Friends joined him, and they named themselves the Society of Jesus (Jesuits).

Each choice of a book, friend, television program, film, web-site, or music will open us to receive beauty, relaxation, truth, understanding, and love, or to enter into emptiness, indifference, and even degradation. We may not always choose a "religious" book or program, but we can make our choices remembering that all of them do change us, even if ever so slightly. We can be lifted up and freed or weighted down.

Choosing: I will reflect on choices I make for relaxation and entertainment that lead me to freedom and peace.

Paying the Price: I may need to give up some choices that interest me, even though they leave me feeling restless and empty.

Praying: I ask for wisdom in my choices today.

To Consider

Kent grew up believing that his older brother was the favorite of his parents. He felt that he could never compete with his sibling's school record or sports abilities. Kent feared comparisons and was quiet and docile, trying not to call attention to himself.

Now in his 40s, Kent refuses invitations from his brother to celebrate family holidays in his brother's house, which is more expensive than anything Kent could ever own. He says that his brother considers himself superior to him. "I don't need him," he tells himself. Kent's children seldom see their cousins.

His belief carries into his other relationships. Because he feels that other people look down on him, he tells himself that they, too, are expendable. He settles for more isolation, less love.

Kent is walking away from the gate to the Community of God. He cannot walk through with the bulk of all that baggage of the past.

Choosing: I will ask myself if I avoid anybody because of past comparisons or because I think I know what others think of me. Am I holding on to any baggage from my childhood?

Paying the Price: Dumping judgments from the past requires courage and sometimes means asking for help.

Praying: Show me any hidden baggage that I need to discard.

TO CONSIDER

To demonstrate a phrase from the Sermon on the Mount one Sunday, a local pastor walked down the center aisle with a large, lighted candle as he proclaimed, "You are the light of the world." Then he began slowly lifting a bushel basket to bring it up and over the flame. A wide-eyed five-year-old exploded with "Uh-oh!" The lesson about the tragedy of hiding our faith, our gifts, under a basket needed to go no further.

Do we need some helpful voices in our lives when we want to hide our faith, our light, because we fear failure or what others may think? Wouldn't it be encouraging if someone would just say "uh-oh" when we want to affirm someone but are afraid she will question our motives? Perhaps "uh-oh" would remind us that we can speak the truth in love to someone even if our words tumble out in some disarray. How about an "uh-oh" when a relationship is hurting and we don't have the courage to apologize for our part in causing pain? "Uh-oh" might call us out of our cowardice to share our faith perspective with another.

We cover light with darkness in many ways. "Uh-oh," is that my choice!

Choosing: I will think of the strengths and faith that I have that can be light for others.

Paying the Price: We are hurt when something precious in us is refused or ignored.

Praying: Reveal more of my light to me.

$\mathcal{T}$rusting in God, Serving in Love

Whenever we open our shell to reveal the pearl of great price, we open ourselves to a greater experience of life. We stand ready to be wrapped in affirmation and love down to the core, to be capable of intimacy. But we also become vulnerable to the hammers of hostility and the scratches of rejection. Our natural fear of suffering can send us scampering back to the "security" of our shells.

The Merchant, however, will search for us and invite us out again.

What makes it possible to live vulnerably? I could say again that the possibility lies in the good news: that our Creating Center loves us individually and unconditionally, that this *Abba* forgives us our trespasses. I could add Jesus' promise: "I will be with you always" (Mt 28:20). I could also recall Jesus' description of how *Abba* cares for us—like the birds of the air and the lilies of the field (Mt 6:26-28).

But another key to living outside of a shell is within us. It is our willingness to take risks that provide the opportunity to grow in trusting Saving Mystery and the

121

above revelations. All risks involve uncertainty, and uncertainty is the price we are asked to pay. Our only security is our faith in the Invisible Hand.

Trusting in God

What does it mean to trust the One-Who-Lives-Within? An answer came to me in a dramatic way many years ago when I was a young Sister teaching at one of our high schools. The practice of our community was to spend the first Sunday of each month in silence, considering our lives from the perspective of death. On one of these "Death Sundays," I was pacing up and down a driveway that ran between the school and a landscape of trees and gardens. As I walked, I held and thought about the notes from my last eight-day retreat.

During that retreat, I had been feeling anxious and didn't know why. I had experienced this kind of "free-floating anxiety" at times in the past. Wandering through our library, I came across a book, *Holiness Is Wholeness*, by psychologist Josef Goldbrunner. As I flipped through it randomly, a passage on trust seemed to leap off the page. I knew that I was far, far away from the kind of trust it described. Yet, something about the message resonated deep within me.

Goldbrunner began with this scripture passage:

> I tell you not to worry about your livelihood,
> what you shall eat or drink or use for clothing. . . .
> Look at the birds in the sky; they don't sow, or reap;
> they gather nothing, yet Our God in heaven feeds
>   them (Mt 6:25-26).

He followed it with these comments:

> This is no rash consolation, implying that Providence will care for the children of God. To interpret it thus means that one has failed to penetrate to its deeper meaning. It is not a word of consolation at all, but a crucial prohibition. The sentence, "I forbid you to worry" does not mean, "I will take your worries upon myself and then all will be well with you." On the contrary, it removes the ultimate safeguards from us; it exposes us to total fear.
>
> We are to live as carefree as the birds. The birds of the air never sow or reap or gather—but we know that not all birds find their grain, that some freeze or die of hunger in the snow.
>
> That is the decisive point. Ultimately it is quite unimportant whether a person dies of hunger or whether she is well or ill. God has not undertaken to see that his disciples fare well in this life. The human situation could not, in fact, be demonstrated more clearly than in this injunction of Christ. It almost makes one dizzy to be forced to look into this fearful abyss. But we are not impelled into this stupefying insecurity simply to sink resignedly into the inevitable darkness. This is falsehood; it is against the intentions of life itself.
>
> In the midst of this fear we are to have the courage to let ourselves go and put our trust in another whom we have never seen, to seek an invisible hand, to believe in a heart that has passed through every one of our fears and now reigns above as Christ the Lord.

> God has promised that whoever serves him will
> not be lost. To let oneself go and, in the very midst
> of fear, to trust another, of whom one knows only
> by faith, is to be redeemed from fear.
>
> Fear calls forth the desire for security, but faith
> demands that the heart should abandon itself to
> the unknown God.
>
> Insofar as we refuse this surrender and fully
> reject faith, we expose ourselves to fear with all
> its imperilments of health.

I was meditating on this passage, copied into my personal notebook, as I walked up and down the driveway on that day of silence. Suddenly I was startled at hearing a *twack* above me. A bird had flown with force into a small, high window of the school. Then it rebounded and fell directly in front of me, just a few inches from my toes. The audio-visual stunned me. I ran back to the nearby convent building and tucked myself in the corner of a small room to let my heart slow down.

Perhaps it is just knocked out, not dead, I thought. So I gingerly went back to the driveway and found the bird—already becoming food for the insects.

For a long time afterward, I feared that something terrible would happen to me. I also knew that I wouldn't be able to meet it with the trust the passage proscribed. Years later, I confided the story and my fear to a wise, older woman, a Sister with whom I was directing retreats. She suggested that the "fall" had already happened as she recalled some of the seriously disturbing circumstances of my childhood that were undoubtedly the cause of the recurring anxiety in me. Something in me knew that she was right.

I have kept that passage beside my bed. It calls me to trust that, no matter what falls I endure, I can reach for that Invisible Hand held out to me. It is a call to trust that the same Hand is extended for others also.

Over and over, Jesus emphasizes that it is faith that saves us. With faith, we can grow in trust.

Believers intellectually profess that God is trustworthy and will keep the promise to be with us always. However, I have frequently heard statements like, "Well, God would never let such a thing happen to us," or, "What have I done that God has given me this illness?" For these people, trust in God means trusting that, if they are good, they will experience no major suffering. But nowhere is this promised. We recognize this as we look at Jesus and all the suffering he endured. *Abba* did not take it away. Jesus, too, had his faith and trust challenged.

I am somewhat closer now to realizing what genuine trust means. I know that it is not something we affirm once and for all and then rest in for the remainder of our lives. We wonder where it is at times and then we find and re-claim it—over and over again. The trust sinks deeper in us as we do so.

When we trust another person, we accept what they say as truthful. We believe that they will not intentionally hurt us. We count on them to make every effort to fulfill their promises to us. But not everyone is to be trusted. Though we can trust God fully, we must make judgments about which human hands we can trust with our pearl. Jesus, himself, said,

> Don't throw your pearls to the pigs.
> If you do,
> they'll just trample them underfoot—
> then turn and tear you to pieces (Mt 7:6).

When we encounter untrustworthy persons, we do not necessarily need to retreat behind our shells again—though consciously doing so for a time may be a prudent move. We may need to keep as much distance as possible from those who will tear into us. Still, our life experience tells us that nothing we can do will keep us from being hurt, ignored, abandoned, or betrayed. When these things happen, we will experience fear, anger, and sadness in full force. Like Jesus, we must accept and feel the pain of these emotions. It is in following this example of Jesus that we will become open to gladness and joy in the future. With trust in an Invisible Hand, we can go through our suffering, knowing that if we die with him, we shall rise with him.

It is this trust in God which allows us to live in freedom—even in suffering. This is, indeed, a pearl of great price.

> You will obtain the freedom of the glory of the children of God.
>
> —Romans 8:21

Serving God and Others

Albert Schweitzer said, "The only ones among you who will be really happy are those who have sought and found how to serve." Jesus said, "The Promised One has not come to be served, but to serve" (Mk 10:45).

Matthew, Mark, and Luke tell stories of the Last Supper, the sharing of bread and wine that we now call eucharist. John's account of the Last Supper, however, does not recall the bread and wine, but another sharing that reveals a deeper meaning of eucharist (Jn 13:2-20).

We are told that garbage and animal dung filled the streets of Jerusalem in Jesus' time. So when the disciples arrived to celebrate Passover, their feet were not only dusty, but filthy. According to the custom of the time, servants would wash the feet of guests before they approached the table. At this meal, however, Jesus took off his own cloak, wrapped a towel around his waist and washed each of the disciple's feet. They were embarrassed. This was work for the lowest in society, not for Jesus, their leader and teacher.

Jesus saw their embarrassment and told them,

"If I, then—your Teacher and Sovereign—have
 washed your feet,
you should wash each other's feet.
I have given you an example,
that you should do as I have done to you."

I imagine the disciples were shocked into silence. They had expected to be first in the Reign of God, but now they were being asked to perform the lowest of tasks. They knew well the command, "Love your neighbor as yourself," but—is this what love of neighbor entails?

Perhaps Jesus' washing of their feet and his command for them to do so unclogged memories of other words they hadn't quite understood;

> "Those who make themselves as humble as this child are the greatest in the kindom of heaven" (Mt 18:4)

or

> "Anyone among you who wishes to be first must serve the needs of all" (Mt 20:27).

They may have remembered, but with greater understanding, the story of the Last Judgment in which the criterion for eternal life is service to the poorest (Mt 25:34-46).

Aware of their consternation, and perhaps with some amusement at the paradox he was presenting, Jesus explains:

> "I tell you all this that my joy may be yours, and your joy may be complete" (Jn 15:11).

Serving is not necessarily a joy in itself. But it explodes with joy when we can serve willingly, freely, from within. In loving service, we enter the Community of God—even here on earth.

When we are ready to emerge from our shells, the Merchant embraces us and we embrace each other as the pearls the Magnificent Jeweler intends us to be. He invites us into the Reign with the invitation:

"Freely have you received, so freely give."